Bad Bet

Written by
Stephen Rickard

I had a bug.

The bug had a red back.

I met a big cat.
I bet the big cat can not get the bug.

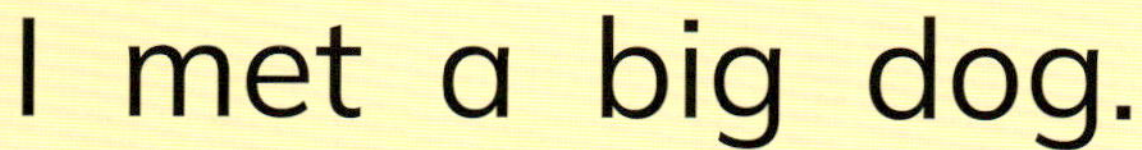

I met a big dog.

I bet the big dog can not get the bug.

The big dog ran at the bug, but it did not get it.

I met a bat.
I bet the bat can not
get the bug.

Bad bet!

The bat **did** get the bug.